Guild

MW01675120

# WOMEN'S MINISTRIES

*I now remind you to stir into flame the gift of God which is within you.*

*—2 Timothy 1:6*

*By Maxine West*
*Women's Division*
*General Board of Global Ministries*

**WOMEN'S MINISTRIES**



*This book is printed on acid-free paper.*

**ISBN 0-687-00080-7**



MANUFACTURED IN THE UNITED STATES OF AMERICA

## CONTENTS

# Our Identity, Call, and Mission

You are so important to the life of the Christian church! You have consented to be among a great and long line of people who have shared the faith and led others in the work of Jesus Christ. We have the church only because over the millennia people like you have caught the vision of God's kingdom and have claimed a place in the faith community to extend God's love to others. You have been called and have committed your unique passions, gifts, and abilities in a position of leadership, and this guide will help you understand some of the elements of that ministry and how it fits within the mission of your church and of The United Methodist Church.

"The mission of the Church is to make disciples of Jesus Christ. Local churches provide the most significant arena through which disciple-making occurs" (*The Book of Discipline of The United Methodist Church, 2004,* ¶120). The church is not only local but also global, and it is for everyone. Our church has an organizational structure through which we work, but it is a living organism as well. Each person is called to ministry by virtue of his or her baptism, and that ministry takes place in all aspects of daily life, not just within the walls of the church. Our *Book of Discipline* describes our mission to proclaim the gospel and to welcome people into the body of Christ, to lead people to a commitment to God through Jesus Christ, to nurture them in Christian living by various means of grace, and to send them into the world as agents of Jesus Christ (¶121). Thus, through you—and many other Christians—this very relational mission continues. (The *Discipline* explains the ministry of all Christians and the essence of servant ministry and leadership in ¶¶125–137.)

## Essential Leadership Functions

Five functions of leadership are essential to strengthen and support the ministry of the church: identifying and supporting leaders as spiritual leaders, discovering current reality, naming shared vision, developing action plans, and monitoring the journey. This Guideline will help you identify these elements and set a course for ministry.

### Lead in the Spirit

Each leader is a spiritual leader and has the opportunity to model spiritual maturity and discipline. John Wesley referred to the disciplines that cultivate a relationship with God as the "means of grace" and suggested several means: prayer, Bible study, fasting, public and private worship, Christian conversation, and acts of mercy. Local church leaders are strongly encouraged to identify their own spiritual practices, cultivate new ones as they grow in their own faith, and model and encourage these practices among their ministry team participants.

### Discover Current Reality

"The way things are" is your current reality. How you organize, who does what, how bills get paid, and plans get made are all building blocks of your current reality. Spend time with people who have been in this ministry and with your committee members to assess their view of how things are. Use "Christian conversation," one of the means of grace, not only to talk to others openly about their understanding of current reality but also to listen for the voice of God regarding your area of ministry.

### Name Shared Vision

"The way things are" is only a prelude to "the way you want things to be." When the church is truly of God, it is the way God would envision it to be. Spend time with your committee and with other leaders in the church to discern the best and most faithful future you can imagine. How can you together identify your role and place in a faithful community that extends itself in its fourfold mission of reaching out and receiving people in the name of God, relating people to God, nurturing them in Christ and Christian living, and sending them forth as ministers into the world? Examine your committee's role and its place in that big picture and try to see yourselves as God's agents of grace and love.

### Develop Action Plans

How do you get from here (your current reality) to there (your shared vision)? As a leader, one of your tasks is to hold in view both what is and what is hoped for so that you can build bridges to the future. These bridges are the interim goals and the action plans needed to accomplish the goals that will make your vision a reality. Remember that God may open up many (or different) avenues to that future, so be flexible and open to setting new goals and accepting new challenges. Action plans that describe how to meet interim goals should be specific, measurable, and attainable. While it is faithful to allow for the wondrous work of God in setting out bold plans, balance that boldness with realism. You and your committee will find information and tips here on developing and implementing the shared vision, the goals toward that vision, and the specific action plans that will accomplish the goals.

### Monitor the Journey

A fifth responsibility of leaders is to keep an eye on how things are going. Setbacks will surely occur, but effective leaders keep moving toward their envisioned future. Not only will you monitor the progress of your committee's action plans to a faithful future but you will also be called to evaluate them in light of the ministry of the rest of the church. Immerse yourself and your plans in God's love and care. Voices from the congregation (both pro and con) may be the nudging of God to shift direction, rethink or plan, or move ahead boldly and without fear. Faithful leaders are attentive to the discernment of the congregation and to the heart of God in fulfilling the mission of the church.

# Getting Started

## Job Description

As president, you work with the Executive Committee to carry out the administrative functions of the unit and provide opportunities for members to fulfill the PURPOSE of United Methodist Women.

## Election and Term of Office

You are elected by the local unit of United Methodist Women for a term of office determined by the unit but limited to four consecutive years. By the *Discipline*, you must be a member of the local congregation of The United Methodist Church.

## Basic Responsibilities of the President

1. To preside at all meetings of the unit and its executive committee.

2. To serve as a member of the church council or on the administrative board or council on ministries where they exist and where provided in the local church's structure.

3. To sign with the secretary all official and legal papers and orders on the treasury.

4. To participate in and encourage the participation of members in regularly scheduled district and conference activities of United Methodist Women and in special enrichment opportunities.

5. To prepare reports as necessary with the elected officers.

6. To share with the church council your plans and programs to keep them informed.

7. To enable the unit and its members to assume appropriate responsibility in the total life of the congregation.

## Special Role of President

1. Participate in the church council (administrative council, administrative board, or other leadership group).

2. Help the executive committee to set goals for its work.

3. Establish and maintain good working relationship with the pastor.

4. Serve as primary contact for district and conference organizations of United Methodist Women.

# Handbook

## What Is United Methodist Women?

The year 2004 marked the 135th Anniversary of United Methodist Women. Since the founding of the first national organization in 1869, The Woman's Foreign Missionary Society of the Methodist Episcopal Church, women have been called to a life of Christian witness, mission outreach, and service. Organizationally, United Methodist Women is the successor to the home and foreign missionary societies and guilds of the eight predecessor denominations that now comprise The United Methodist Church. It is:

- an organization of lay women centered in relationship with God through Jesus Christ.
- an integral part of The United Methodist Church, authorized by General Conference to organize units in local congregations. "In every local church there shall be an organized unit of United Methodist Women." (the *Book of Discipline* 2004, ¶256.4).
- focused on ministries with women, children, and youth (See Policy Statement: Ministries With Women and Ministries With Children and Youth).
- rooted in mission and involved in mission programs locally and globally.
- pledged to provide financial support for mission through undesignated giving.
- a multiracial and multicultural organization committed to inclusiveness; and
- a community of women who nurture and encourage one another in their spiritual growth and personal development.

## What Is the PURPOSE?

United Methodist Women is a community of women whose PURPOSE is to know God and to experience freedom as whole persons through Jesus Christ; to develop a creative supportive fellowship; and to expand concepts of mission through participation in the global ministries of the church.

## What Is the Emblem?

"I now remind you to stir into flame the gift of God which is within you…" (2 Timothy 1:6). Inspired by a passage of Scripture from 2 Timothy 1:6, the emblem of United Methodist Women symbolizes the organization. The cross and flame are ancient symbols of the Church and appear on The United Methodist Church emblem. Both remind us of our PURPOSE of growing in our understanding of and willingness to participate in the global ministries of the Church. The shape is fluid and free-flowing, suggesting change and mobility. The women who came before us, serving the Church at home and in other countries, were at the forefront of movements for change. Always aware of the times, we move into the twenty-first century aware of the opportunities and obligations of discipleship. We are a group of Christian women with many gifts who are unified by our Spirit. We participate in God's mission in all areas of life.

## Who Is a Member?

Membership is open to any woman who indicates her desire to belong and to participate in the outreach mission of the church through the organization. Over one million lay women have chosen to be members of United Methodist Women.

## What Is Expected of a Member?

When a woman chooses to be a member of United Methodist Women, she is expected to:

- attend unit meetings, and participate in various events, projects, issues, and concerns of the Women's Division
- support global mission programs through undesignated giving
- participate in local community concerns and issues affecting the lives of women and children
- accept leadership responsibility
- join in intercessory prayer on behalf of others
- keep informed of the ongoing concerns and programs of United Methodist Women and the Women's Division
- study and use resources developed for United Methodist Women, including the *Program Book, Response* magazine, Bible studies, and spiritual growth resources
- engage in critical analysis and active listening while remaining open to differing perceptions and diverse views
- participate in the Reading Program
- make suggestions and recommendations for programs, resources, and activities that increase awareness and understanding of global issues concerning women and children.

We are organized for mission! We are not a group to be joined lightly where membership has no meaning. UNITED METHODIST WOMEN is a missional organization, with responsibilities to all members in each unit and for a worldwide program of mission outreach. Our hallmarks are mission, inclusiveness, continuity from the past, flexibility to meet ever changing needs, provision for leadership opportunities and financial support, and a willingness to move out into new and adventurous paths. (*United Methodist Women: In the Middle of Tomorrow* by Barbara E. Campbell)

# How Do We Organize a Unit?

The Constitution and Bylaws of United Methodist Women provide for three types of units: local church-based units; charge and cluster units; and district units. These three types of units offer members the opportunity for participation in mission in a variety of settings. (See Constitution and Bylaws 2005-2008, Local, Article I, Section 1-9 for organizational information.)

- Most of the membership of United Methodist Women is in units based in local churches.
- A **charge** or **cluster** unit may be formed by women from more than one church. This type of unit is usually formed when the number of women from a single church is too small to carry out the basic structure.
- A **district** unit may be formed by women from different churches who choose to meet in locations other than a local church, such as on a college campus, in a retirement community, or in other locations.

A local unit should be organized as soon as possible after the formation of a new United Methodist congregation. Special efforts should also be made to organize or reorganize units in established churches currently without units. The District Executive Committee of United Methodist Women is prepared to give assistance to a local group interested in organizing a unit. All women in the congregation should be invited to a meeting designed to explain the organization and its PURPOSE. The agenda might include the following:

**Sample Agenda for Meeting**

1. PURPOSE of United Methodist Women
- history
- programs, goals, and vision
- policy statement and programmatic thrust on Ministries With Women and Ministries with Children and Youth
- opportunities for nurture, study, reflection, and action
- relationship to Women's Division and the General Board of Global Ministries

2. Meaning of Membership
- voluntary and intentional
- expectations of a members

3. Organization Structure
- basic
- expanded
- minimum functions

4. Relationships Within the Local Congregation
5. Connectional Relationships to the District, Conference, and the Women's Division
- financial
- programmatic

6. Function and Work of the Committee on Nominations
7. Time for Questions and Comments

During this meeting, the following decisions should be made:
1. Approve recommendation for organizing a unit.
2. Elect temporary Committee on Nominations (three persons) to nominate the first slate of officers. Elect one of the three to serve as chairperson. This committee is dissolved at the completion of this one task. A new Committee on Nominations will be elected with the slate of new officers and will assume the nominations responsibility.
3. Decide on organizational structure and slate of officers to be nominated.
4. Set the date, time, and place for the organizational meeting and service of celebration.

You will want to have print and audiovisual resources available for review during this exploratory meeting. The following resources can be ordered from the Service Center, Cincinnati, Ohio:
- *Response* magazine
- "Who Are United Methodist Women?" flyer
- *Local Handbook for United Methodist Women*
- *Financial Handbook for United Methodist Women*
- *A Guide to Program Planning*
- *Mission: Responding To God's Grace—A Policy Statement on Giving*
- Current Program Book for United Methodist Women
- "United Methodist Women in Mission" brochure
- *A Policy Statement: Ministries with Women and Ministries with Children and Youth*
- Current spiritual growth study materials
- The Prayer Calendar
- *Annual Report of the Women's Division*
- Reading Program brochure

## Organizational Meeting and Celebration

The district mission coordinator for membership outreach and nurture, district president, one of the other district or conference officers, or a director or staff member of the Women's Division residing in the area may preside at the organizational meeting. This meeting should be a happy event, a time of celebration, a time of rejoicing and thanksgiving. Prior to the event, the person presiding should request a Certificate of Organization from the Deputy General Secretary, Women's Division, Room 1504, 475 Riverside Drive, New York, NY 10115.

A suggested agenda for the organizational meeting includes:
1. Greetings and meditation
2. Purpose and expectations of meeting

3. Election and installation of officers
4. Presentation of Certificate of Organization
5. Service of Celebration

Immediately following the meeting, be sure that the following information is sent to the director at: The Service Center, 7820 Reading Road, Caller No. 1800, Cincinnati, OH 45222-1800.

1. The name and address of the local church in which the unit is being organized.
2. The name and address of the president and the secretary of program resources.

## How Is the Local Unit Structured?

Each local unit can choose one of three structures to meet its needs: Minimum Functions structure, Basic structure, or Expanded structure.

1. **Minimum Functions** structure is for units with fifteen or fewer active members. Two or more women are elected to carry out the functions of administration, finance, program, record keeping, and nominations.

2. **Basic structure** consists of a president, vice president, secretary, treasurer, secretary of program resources, and the chair of the Committee on Nominations.

3. **Expanded structure** consists of the basic structure plus one or more mission coordinators; spiritual growth, social action, education and interpretation, and membership nurture and outreach chairs.

### Committees

The committee structure of the local unit shall include an Executive Committee and a Committee on Nominations. The Executive Committee is elected by the unit and carries out the following functions:

- administration
- program planning for mission
- finances
- record-keeping.

The pastor of the church is a member of the local unit and its Executive Committee. When the Executive Committee meets, the president presides.

In the *Minimum Function structure,* the Executive Committee includes:

- president
- one or more additional officers

In the *Basic structure,* the Executive Committee is elected by the unit and includes:

- president
- vice-president
- secretary
- treasurer
- secretary of program resources
- chairperson of the committee on nominations.

In the *Expanded structure,* the Executive Committee includes any other officers elected by the unit as well as Subgroup and Circle leaders. For information on job responsibilities of elected leaders see the *Handbook Focus on Local Units 2005-2008.*

### Other Committees

A local unit may choose to have a Program Committee, Finance Committee, and a Membership and Nurture Committee to help implement the PURPOSE.

In a unit with a basic structure, the Executive Committee serves as the Program Committee, the Finance Committee, and the Membership, Nurture, and Outreach Committee. When it meets as the Program Committee, the vice-president chairs the meeting. When it meets as a Finance Committee, the treasurer presides. As the Membership, Nurture and Outreach Committee, the mission coordinator of Membership, Nurture and Outreach chairs the meeting.

Units with an expanded structure may also operate in the same way, or they may choose to name separate committees. Refer to *The Handbook Focus on Local Units* for suggested representation on these committees.

### Subgroups and Circles

Units with basic structures and expanded structures may include subgroups or circles. These subgroups or circles are created when a unit is large enough and members want to focus on special mission needs and interests in smaller groups. The nature of subgroups determines their membership and the length of time they exist.

Subgroups and circles enrich and increase the effectiveness of other programs of the unit. They provide greater flexibility for individuals to participate, to feel nurtured, and to develop leadership skills. Members can belong to one or more subgroups or circles. When different small groups meet at various times and places and focus on different concerns and issues, a unit can be more inclusive. The more choices your unit offers, the greater the opportunity for more women from a variety of backgrounds to be involved.

## What Are the Functions of the Unit?

Certain functions are basic to the life of the unit. Some are assigned by Bylaw to certain committees. Others may be assigned to individuals or task groups. These include:

- goal setting
- program planning
- budget building
- interpretation of need for and use of funds
- resource selection
- leadership training and development
- membership cultivation and recruitment
- publicity and public relations
- evaluation and data reporting.

Each local unit shall (1) determine the structure it needs in order to do its most effective work in implementing the PURPOSE; (2) hold a minimum of four meetings of the total membership; and (3) make a financial commitment for the mission program of United Methodist Women.

## Units in Federated Churches

### Guidelines for Units in Federated Churches

Some units are in federated churches. A federated church is a local church that unites two or more congregations, each of which continues its own denominational ties. A unit in a federated church maintains ties to two or more denominational women's organizations. In calculating the membership of the group, one should either report the total number of unit members, divided by the number of denominations represented, or ask individual members to designate their denomination and report accordingly. Units that choose to be related to United Methodist Women:

- Subscribe to the PURPOSE.
- Use an organizational structure that is flexible.
- Recognize membership in the following ways:
  - attendance at meetings
  - undesignated mission giving for global mission
  - intercessory prayer
  - meaningful community involvement

leadership responsibility

participation in the various events, projects, issues, and concerns of the Women's Division.

- Participate in undesignated mission giving as well as designated mission giving (allocating the finances and resources equally among the various denominational women's groups).
- Use resources of the different women's groups, such as magazines, program and study books, and leadership skills of individuals.
- Explore organizational relationships with the denominations that are represented. Participate in as many denominational opportunities as possible beyond the local unit.

## What Is the Scope of the Program?

The PURPOSE and program of United Methodist Women have evolved out of a history of more than a century of women whose primary concern has been mission. The needs of women and children that motivated women in the predecessor organizations during the early nineteenth century still threaten the well-being of women and families today: lack of quality education for women, affordable health care, insufficient housing, racial discrimination, economic disparities between women and men, and unemployment among women and racial or ethnic minorities. The total program United Methodist Women encompasses:

- mission education
- spiritual growth
- social action
- focus on the needs of women and children.

Through its program of mission, United Methodist Women seek to be:

- followers of Jesus Christ living their faith in acts of justice and love
- catalysts for needed change
- mobilizers of human and material resources
- creators of new arenas of participation throughout the church and the world.

Through special programs and emphases like the Campaign for Children Phase III and Mission Today, United Methodist Women are provided opportunities to advocate for good public schools and the rights of children and to participate in a number of projects related to national mission institutions across the country.

The efforts of thousands of United Methodist Women in local units across the country are making the world a safer place for all children to live, grow, learn, and develop into mature individuals. Some ways that United Methodist Women can continue to advocate for the rights of children include:

- observance of the Children's Sabbath

- participating in United Methodist Women Campaign for Children, Phase III, Public Education
- supporting the Rugmark Campaign and other similar efforts aimed at stopping business and labor practices that exploit children in the production of consumer goods
- support efforts to ban landmines that have inflicted enormous pain and suffering on hundred of thousands of children over the last several decades
- become mentors for teen women, encouraging their full participation in United Methodist Women.

There are nearly 10,000 teen and college or university women among the membership of United Methodist. Most of these young women participate in United Methodist Women as members of units organized in local churches. Many teens and college or university women attend meetings alongside older women. Some have their own circles and subgroups that relate to the local unit. Consult the Membership Campaign Packet (#2600) to learn how your unit can organize a teen, college or university circle or subgroup in your unit.

Other programs and program suggestions are available in the annual Program Book and through *Response* magazine, leaflets, study guides, resource packets, the annual Report of the Women's Division, and the United Methodist Women's World-Wide Web Pages.

## How Is the Organization Financed?

The program of United Methodist Women is mission—mission that affirms the wholeness of the gospel and our commitment to proclaim that gospel. Giving for mission is rooted in the long history of the organization. Intentional giving for mission is contemporary—about $19 million in undesignated giving through the Women's Division annually expresses the commitment of women today.

> Understanding the total program as mission becomes very important as funds are received and disbursed. Without mission education, advocacy for the oppressed does not take place. Without a continual growth in Christian faith, social involvement becomes shallow. Without a solid supportive community, women are unable to care for their own needs and the needs of others. Without a clear understanding of the PURPOSE of United Methodist Women by the church, the entire mission of the church suffers. (*With Unveiled Face* by Theressa Hoover)

United Methodist Women have always been generous in giving for mission needs. When funds from United Methodist Women reach the Women's Division, they are considered either "undesignated" or "designated."

Undesignated giving provides funds to which all mission programs have access, and they equalize the financial burden for mission in any given area. Undesignated giving is the basic support of all mission programs related to the organization. There are five channels of undesignated giving: Pledge to Mission, Special Mission Recognition, Gift to Mission, Gift in Memory, and World Thank Offering.

United Methodist Women also have three channels of designated giving that allow for (a) the desire of some donors to make special gifts for specific programs or projects over and above their undesignated giving and (b) the occasional need for special funds in international and national mission programs. Designated giving channels include: Call to Prayer and Self-Denial, Supplementary Gifts, and Assembly Offering. For more complete information about funds and the channels of giving through United Methodist Women, see the *Financial Handbook 2005-2008*.

As president, you will want to work with the unit in establishing a budget. Local unit budgets are supported by individual pledges and gifts or some fundraising activities. Pledge to Mission and other undesignated money sent to the Women's Division becomes the basis of the Division's annual budget. Money is disbursed according to the budget determined by the unit for:

1. Pledge to mission for support of the work of the Women's Division through the General Board of Global Ministries. These funds are sent to the district treasurer who forwards them to the conference treasurer. The conference treasurer sends these funds to the Women's Division treasurer. Included in the pledge are administration and membership development funds for district, conference, and jurisdiction organizations.

2. Administration and membership development for local unit needs.

3. Mission locally, support of ecumenical community programs, Church Women United, World Fellowship for Methodist and Uniting Church Women activities, task groups (if needed) and local programs not a part of the General Board of Global Ministries program.

As president of the unit, you might be asked why there is a separate channel of giving for United Methodist Women. There are legal, functional, and philosophical reasons for maintaining a separate channel of giving for United Methodist Women.

*Legal Reason.* From the *Book of Discipline*: "All undesignated funds channeled to the Women's Division shall be appropriated by the division."

*Functional Reason*. The "Giving for Mission" chart displays the organizational and procedural differences in the use of funds from a local United Methodist Church—offerings by the congregation through World Service and Advance specials, and offerings by United Methodist Women through Pledge to Mission and special offerings. All are essential to the mission and ministry of the church.

*Philosophical Reason*. United Methodist Women preserves the historical concerns of women organized for mission: the role of women in church, the role of women in cultures around the world, ministries with children, concerns for the oppressed and dispossessed. The organization owns and assumes responsibility for financial support of mission programs and projects around the world. In addition, appropriation of funds by the Women's Division is guided by the PURPOSE of United Methodist Women.

## GIVING FOR MISSION

| | Local Church | | Unit of United Methodist Women | |
|---|---|---|---|---|
| **Avenues of Giving** | **World Service** | **Advance Specials** | **Pledge to Mission** | **Supplementary Gifts** |
| **Fund:** | Basic undesignated benevolence fund of The United Methodist Church | Program of General Church for designated giving | International undesignateded giving for mission through UNITED METHODIST WOMEN | Official channel for designated giving through UNITED METHODIST WOMEN |
| **Given by:** | Local Churches | Congregations, Sunday school classes, individual members of local church | Local Units, UNITED METHODIST WOMEN | Individuals and Units desiring to designate some special gift |
| **Routing:** | Conference Treasurer, General Council on Finance and Administration, Boards and agencies of The United Methodist Church, including General Board of Global Ministries | Conference Treasurer, General Council on Finance and Administration, General Board of Global Ministries | District Treasurer, Conference Treasurer<br><br>Women's Division, General Board of Global Ministries | District Treasurer, Conference Treasurer<br><br>Women's Division, General Board of Global Ministries |
| **Used for:** | Budget for boards' and agencies' operation; for two program divisions and four program departments of General Board of Global Ministries | To designated project free of administration costs | Historic concerns of women organized for mission; most central, the needs of women and children | To designated project, free of administration costs |

## How Are We Part of the Connection?

Like the United Methodist Church, the organization of United Methodist Women has district, conference, and jurisdiction organizations. These organized bodies are determined by geography. A district is the smallest area and a jurisdiction the largest area. There is also a national policy-making body named the Women's Division of the General Board of Global Ministries, the national mission agency of The United Methodist Church. (See The Connections of United Methodist Women chart on page 21.)

### The District

Your unit's most immediate link is to the district organization. District officers connect your unit with the conference officers. A district officer will make regular contact with your unit to share information and to provide support within the organization.

You and the members of all the units in your district are part of your district organization. The district holds at least one event each year: an annual meeting featuring a program that is reflective of the PURPOSE and includes a business session. As president of your unit, you will want to know when and where the next district annual meeting will be held. Plan to attend along with other members of the unit.

### The Conference

The conference organization of United Methodist Women connects your district organization with the Women's Division. Conference officers are elected from the members of the United Methodist Women belonging to churches in your conference.

You and the members of all the units in your conference are part of the conference organization of United Methodist Women. Your conference has at least one business meeting a year, the annual meeting. It is usually held in conjunction with a program that interprets the PURPOSE of United Methodist Women. At this event, you will meet women from across the conference, hear special speakers, and have an opportunity to participate in workshops on mission education as well as skills training.

Each conference sponsors at least one School of Christian Mission annually. The schools offer a chance for members to grow spiritually and relationally and to broaden leadership skills. Your conference may also sponsor other mission events such as retreats, seminars, and workshops.

## The Jurisdiction

The structure and role of the Jurisdiction Organization is different from the structure and role of the other parts of United Methodist Women. The jurisdiction "Executive Committee" is called the Core Planning Group. Its task is to provide assistance with mission education training and interpretation to the conference organization.

Once every four years, in the spring of the year the General Conference meets, the Jurisdiction Core Planning Group holds a special quadrennial meeting open to all United Methodist Women in the jurisdiction. The purpose of this event is the election of officers and directors to serve on the Women's Division for the next four years. Mission education and spiritual development are important elements of this meeting.

## The Women's Division

The directors of the Women's Division are volunteers elected every four years. The Division is the official policy-making body for United Methodist Women. This representative body develops resources and shapes policies and programs for the organization.

The Women's Division is responsible for disbursing funds that assist important mission programs and projects around the world, especially those for women, children, and youth. Comprised primarily of women who belong to units like yours, the Women's Division is a resource for United Methodist Women throughout the organization.

Your local or district unit as well as all local or district units benefit from our connectional system. As part of the connection, your local unit can convey its concerns, ideas, funds, and evaluations to the Women's Division. In return, your unit receives resources, skills development, and numerous opportunities to participate in spiritual growth retreats, workshops, and leadership training events.

## The Connections of United Methodist Women

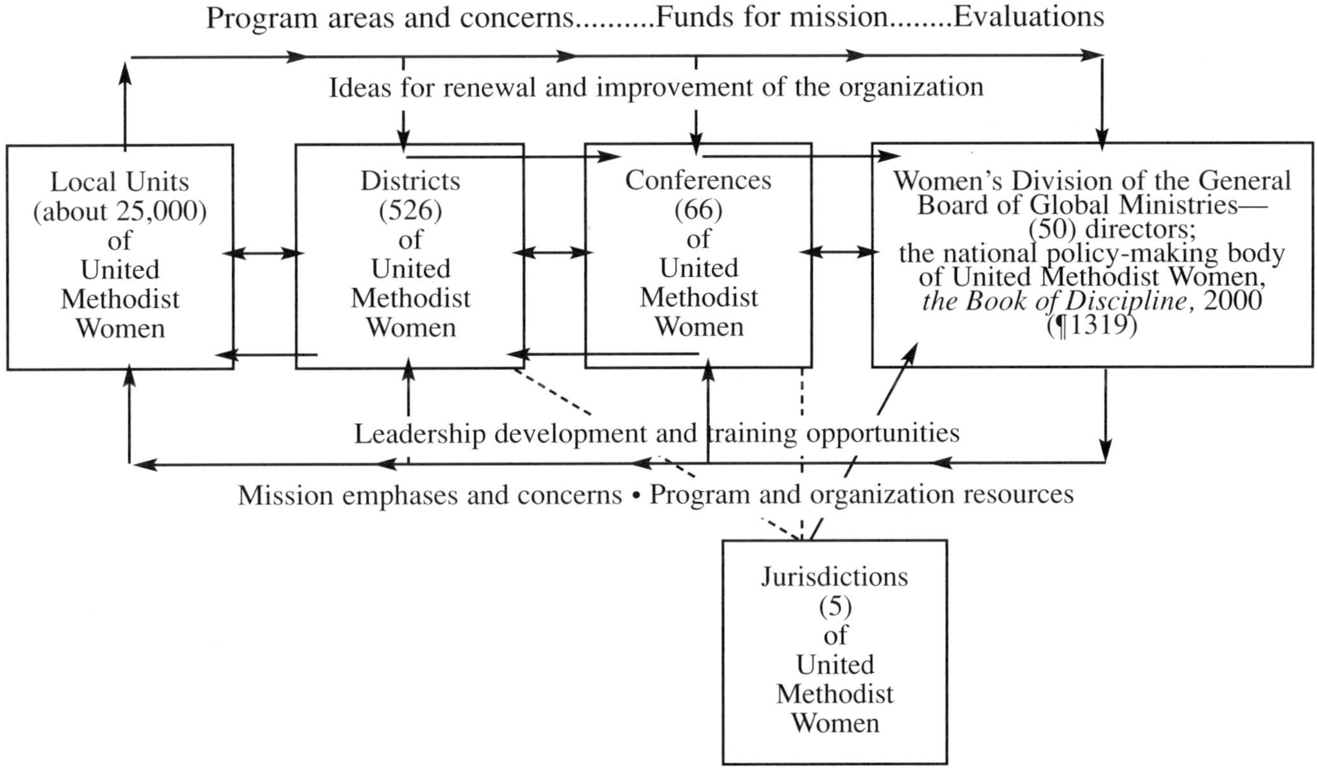

# What Are the Responsibilities of the Women's Division?

**Responsibilities of the Women's Division**

1. To recommend program and policies to United Methodist Women.
2. To interpret the role and responsibility of the division in fulfilling the mission of Christ and the Church.
3. To provide resources and opportunities for women that enrich their spiritual life and increase their knowledge and understanding of the needs of the world and their responsibility in meeting those needs.
4. To secure funds through the channels of United Methodist Women for the support of the program of the Church through the General Board of Global Ministries, with special concerns for the needs of women and children.
5. To project plans specially directed toward leadership development of women through appropriate planning with the other units of the board.
6. To strengthen the Church's challenge to women to enlist in the diaconate as missionaries and deaconesses.
7. To enlist women in activities that have a moral and religious significance for the public welfare and that contribute to the establishment of a just global society.
8. To work with the other agencies of the Church and community in areas of common concern and responsibility. A United Nations Office shall be maintained in cooperation with the General Board of Church and Society.
9. To give visible evidence of oneness in Christ by uniting in fellowship and service with other Christians (including the World Federation of Methodist and Uniting Church Women, Church Women United, and other similar groups) thereby strengthening the ecumenical witness and program of the Church.
10. To formulate concepts of contemporary mission.

(From the *Book of Discipline*, 2004, ¶1318)

# Resources and Tools for Local Units

United Methodist Women have many resources to help in fulfilling the PURPOSE. Some are for elected leaders, others for the entire membership. Below is list of resources essential for every local unit.

### Resources for Elected Leaders and Members

#### For Elected Leaders

- *The Book of Discipline of The United Methodist Church,* 2004. (Available from Cokesbury; call toll-free 1-800-672-1789.) This book is a statement of rules and regulations governing The United Methodist Church and all its agencies, as approved by the General Conference. *The Book of Discipline* includes the constitution of United Methodist Women (local, district, conference, and jurisdiction versions) and the constitution, responsibilities, and organization of the Women's Division. It also contains historical and theological material and the current Social Principles of The United Methodist Church.
- *The Book of Resolutions of The United Methodist Church,* 2004. (Available from Cokesbury; see above.) Official United Methodist Church position statements on a variety of social issues as approved by General Conference.
- *Ceremonies III* (#2575; $2.50). A collection of worship resources for United Methodist Women including services for installation of officers, a memorial service, a Pledge Service, services on the Campaign for Children, and the Charter for Racial Justice.
- *Constitution and Bylaws 2005-2008* (English #2824; Spanish #3962; $3.50 each; 5 or more, $2.80 each). All United Methodist Women's organizations—at the local, district, conference, and jurisdiction levels—have specific instructions about their roles, responsibilities, and relationships to other United Methodist organizations, boards, and agencies. This resource describes these and is essential to your office.
- *Financial Handbook 2005-2008* (English #3726; Spanish #4597; $4.00 each; 5 or more, $3.20 each). This book is a must for treasurers. Other officers will also find information important to understanding our organization.
- *Handbook for United Methodist Women: Focus On Local Units 2005-2008* (English #2894; Spanish #3963; Korean #1824; $4.50 each; 5 or more, $3.60 each). This is the book that is in your hands right now. Every elected officer should have her own copy.

- *Program Book for United Methodist Women* (English and Spanish, published annually. See the *Catalog* for current price.) A collection of program suggestions for United Methodist Women on a variety of mission topics, including a Quiet Day Service, a Pledge Service, and a World Thank Offering service. Check the *Service Center Catalog* for current titles.
- *PURPOSE of United Methodist Women* (English/Spanish #4421; Korean #1733; $1.50). A poster with the words of our PURPOSE in English on one side and Spanish on the reverse. Printed separately in Korean.
- *Service Center Catalog*. This annual catalog lists printed and audiovisual mission resources available from the General Board of Global Ministries. All current materials produced especially for United Methodist Women are listed in it.

### For Elected Leaders and Members

- *Acting Out Our Conversion* (English #1721, $1.50; Spanish #3814, 65¢). This booklet describes the theological basis of our PURPOSE and comes with a study guide.
- *Annual Report, General Board of Global Ministries* (published annually). Describes the work of all program units of the General Board of Global Ministries for the previous year.
- *Ecumenical Mission Studies*. Each year, Friendship Press of the National Council of the Churches of Christ, USA produces printed and audiovisual materials on two different topics, one a geographical mission theme and one a general mission theme. These are introduced in our denomination through our Schools of Christian Mission. Check the *Service Center Catalog* for current titles and descriptions.
- *How to Contact Your Members of Congress* (#5126) and *How to Visit Your Members of Congress* (#5127; both free for postage and handling). These two leaflets give specifics on how to speak to your legislators on behalf of women and children.
- *I Was Sick and You Visited Me* (English #1263; Spanish #2830; $2.50). An updated guide on visitation ministry.
- *Invitation to Membership* (English #5365; Spanish #5378; Korean #5688; free for postage and handling). A brochure that introduces new members to United Methodist Women.
- *Yes! Count Me In! New Member Campaign Packet* (English #2600; Spanish #2612; Korean #2619; $3.95). Contains tools needed for bringing new members into United Methodist Women.
- *Material Resources for Mission Catalog* (#2579; see *Service Center*

*Catalog* for price). A listing of opportunities for giving material resources that will be distributed to projects and for emergency relief.

- *Ministries with Women and Ministries with Children and Youth: A Gift for the Whole Church* (English #1892; Spanish #1893; Korean #2580; 30¢ ). A policy statement of the Women's Division, with a study guide, that reviews the position of women, children, and youth in our society to discern our ongoing mission.
- *Mission: Responding to God's Grace, A Policy Statement on Giving of the Women's Division* (English #2581; Spanish #2582; Korean #2583; 50¢). A policy statement that stresses the biblical and theological reasons for giving. This booklet includes a study guide.
- *My Date Book* (published annually; see *Service Center Catalog* for price). Program calendar in a purse-size booklet.
- *New World Outlook* ($15 a year, $26 for two-year subscription; published bi-monthly). As the mission magazine of The United Methodist Church, it reports on the work of the General Board of Global Ministries and the ecumenical mission of the church. Special combination subscription price with *Response:* 1 year, $20; 2 years, $36.
- *One Million Plus—United Methodist Women* (English #5091; Spanish #5115; Korean #5260; free for postage and handling). A colorful leaflet that describes United Methodist Women as a community that is unique, faithful, purposeful, supportive, and global.
- *Prayer Calendar* (published annually; see *Service Center Catalog* for price). A daily guide to prayer for mission workers and mission projects in the United States and around the world. Includes names, addresses, birthdays, special prayers, daily scripture readings, maps, and pages of special interest.
- *Children's Prayer Calendar* (published annually). Pocket calendars with missionary children's birthdays and addresses. Set of 8: #2516, $8.00.
- *Reading Program* Booklet (published annually). Free except for postage and handling. This booklet describes Reading Program plans and books. Books are listed under each of the four mission emphases. A new list is published each year.
- *Response* ($15/year, $27 for two-year subscription; published 11 times a year). *Response* magazine is the official program journal for United Methodist Women. It is essential for every leader and for every member. Regular reading of this magazine increases one's understanding of the current program and concerns of the Women's Division and of United Methodist Women in global mission. The focus is on women, children, and youth. In addition, there are organizational and program aids for elected leaders.

- *Report of the Women's Division* (published annually; see *Service Center Catalog* for current price). This annual report of the Women's Division updates the ways in which United Methodist Women continue their heritage of mission work with women, children, and youth. It is a good resource for programming and for understanding how funds are distributed within the organization of United Methodist Women.
- *Spiritual Growth Study* (English, Spanish, and Korean; published annually; see *Service Center Catalog* for current title and price). Published by the Women's Division, this book is one of the three annual mission studies, written espe-cially for United Methodist Women. It includes a study guide.
- *20 Questions* (pamphlet, English #5436; Spanish #5557; Korean #5646; free for postage and handling). Answers basic questions about United Methodist Women.
- *United Methodist Women in Mission* (English #2139; Spanish #2143; Korean #2182; 25¢). This is a resource for new members, pastors, and all United Methodist Women. Designed with brilliant sunburst colors, it expands on *One Million Plus—United Methodist Women* and includes the biblical basis for our long heritage of mission.
- *Where the Money Goes* Packet (updated annually; #1371, $1.15). A resource for interpreting how money is spent in the organization.
- *Why Have a Charter for Racial Justice Policies?* (English #5297; Spanish #5338; free for postage and handling). Contains the Charter for Racial Justice Policies for United Methodist Women, which has also been adopted as a resolution of The United Methodist Church. See below for a description of the video companion to this resource.
- *Why Should I Get Involved in Social Issues? A Call to Action for United Methodist Women* (English #5132; Spanish #5196; free for postage and handling).

**Resources on History**

- *By My Spirit: The Story of Methodist Protestant Women in Mission* by Ethel Born (#1312; $3.95). An historical overview of Methodist Protestant women in mission in Japan, China, India, and the United States.
- *They Went out Not Knowing: 100 Women in Mission* (#3806; $3.25). A collection of 100 biographical sketches of women in United Methodist Women and its predecessor organizations from 1869 to 1985.
- *This Is Our Song: Employed Women in the United Methodist Tradition* by Ann Fagan (#3718; $3.95) covers the years 1921 to 1972.
- *Speaking Out in the Public Space: An Account of the Section of Christian Social Relations* by Peggy Billings (#2517; $5.00) covers the years 1968 to 1984.

**Resources on History: Out of Print**

The three books listed below are out of print. However, they are available on the United Methodist Women's History Web Site (http://gbgm-umc.org/umw/history) and on CD-ROM. The CD-ROM can be purchased from Service Center (#2829, $40).

- *In the Middle of Tomorrow* by Barbara E. Campbell. Provides a comprehensive examination of the Women's Division.
- *Legacy for the Future: The History of Christian Social Relations in the Woman's Division of Christian Service 1940-1968* by Thelma Stevens. Details the history of Methodist women's work for justice during this twenty-eight-year period.
- *To a Higher Glory: The Growth and Development of Black Women Organized for Mission in the Methodist Church 1940-1968.*

## Audiovisuals

- *The Charter for Racial Justice—A History* (#4451; $5.00) is a video illustrating the history of the Women's Division's work on the Charter for Racial Justice. This is an excellent resource for all levels of United Methodist Women and for the general church as well. It includes a script/guide (#4736; $1.00).
- *Empowering Viewers for Music Videos* (#2507; $15.00) is a 22-minute video that explores the impact of music videos and empowers youth and adults to become informed viewers and agents of change.
- *Journey of Your Mission Dollar* (English #2626; $15.00) is a video that traces undesignated gifts as they move from local units to the Women's Division. This revised version illustrates a variety of mission programs.
- *Giving: A Gift of God—Grace.* This video features women's witness on "what United Methodist Women has meant to me" as it explores the idea of giving as a response to God's goodness. (Available from EcuFilm—See below. Rental: $12.50; Sale: $25.00.)
- *Mission Magazine* (video). Each summer, this video features the three annual mission studies to be introduced in the Regional Schools of Christian Mission. See the *Service Center Catalog* for current information.
- *Response on Cassette.* Highlighted articles from each issue are available on a subscription basis as follows: (a) $15 per year (11 issues) for persons with visual impairment; (b) $35 per year for groups (conferences, audiovisual libraries, districts) that wish either to make additional copies for persons with visual impairment or to make copies available on loan. If sighted individuals wish to subscribe to this service, it is at the $35 rate.
- *United Methodist Women's Campaign for Children: To Love in Deed.* A 30-minute video (with study guide) showing two successful outreach programs for children. (Available from EcuFilm, 810 Twelfth Avenue South, Nashville, TN 37203. Call toll free: 1-800-251-4091. Rental $10.00; sale $15.00.)

## What Is the Service Center

Your main source of printed and audiovisual resources is the Service Center. The Service Center is the distribution center for literature, audiovisual resources, and books of the General Board of Global Ministries. All materials prepared especially for United Methodist Women are available there and are listed in the annual Service Center Catalog. A copy of the catalog is sent to all local Secretaries of Program Resources whose names are in the Service Center data bank.

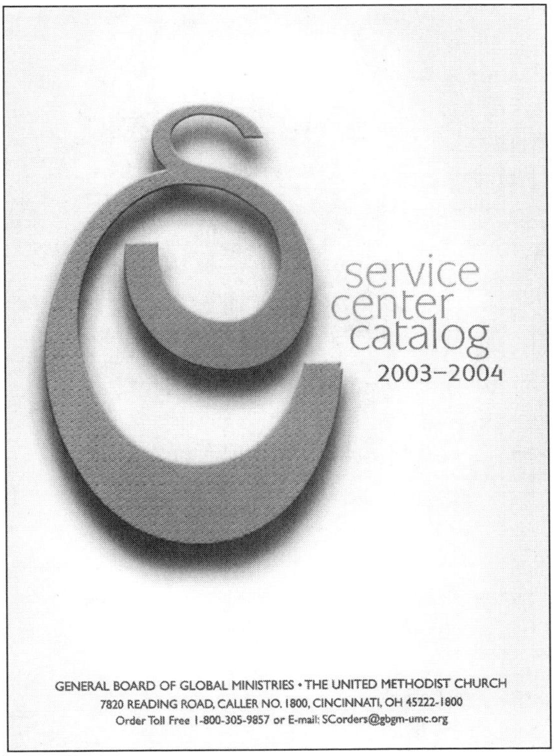


All inquires and questions related to resources should be addressed to:

The Service Center
General Board of Global Ministries
7820 Reading Road, Caller No. 1800
Cincinnati, OH 45222-1800

The Women's Division produces resources in English, Spanish, and Korean. Check the current catalog for prices and postage and handling charges for materials. As the president, you will want to ensure that the secretary of program resources or someone designated to carry out that function has a catalog and understands how to order resources from the Service Center. The Service Center's toll-free number for placing orders is 1-800-305-9857. You may also correspond by fax at 513-761-3722, or by calling 513-761-2100.

It is important that your secretary send the names of the newly elected president and secretary of program resources to the Service Center annually. You will not want to miss receiving materials that come to the unit from the Women's Division.

### What Is *Response* Magazine?

*Response,* "The Voice of Women in Mission," is the official program journal for United Methodist Women and is published eleven times a year. It is essential reading for every leader and every member of the organization. Regular reading of *Response* increases one's understanding of the current program and concerns of the Women's Division and United Methodist Women in global mission. The focus of the magazine is on women, children, and youth. You will also find organizational tools and program aids and suggestions.

*Response*'s colorful photos and lively copy tell the mission story of United Methodist Women and stir readers to solidarity and action with women, youth, and children of the world. *Response* carries a message of faith and hope, a call to justice, and the new reign of God.

As president of the unit, you will want to subscribe to *Response*. A subscription is $15 per year and $27 for two years. It is also important that all elected officers of the unit have a subscription to *Response*.

### Opportunities for Growth and Training

1. Officer Training and Leadership Development opportunities are available to local unit leaders in a variety of ways—district officer training days, cluster meetings, officer time at Conference Schools of Christian Mission, and so forth. Check with your district president to discover what kinds of opportunities are available for your local unit.

2. Schools of Christian Mission or Mission Education Events are held annually in each conference. They are one of the strongest links of the total women's organization. The date and place for each school is listed in *Response* in the Spring.

3. District and Conference Annual Meetings are held each year. They combine a business meeting and a program for members of United Methodist Women in the district or conference in keeping with the PURPOSE and work of the organization and the Women's Division. The meetings are open to all members of United Methodist Women. (For more details about these meetings, see the Handbook or contact your district president.)

4. Other special events are sponsored frequently by district and conference United Methodist Women. These may be retreats, seminars, workshops, financial promotion events, or one of several other experiences. The district president is your contact for up-to-date information about such events.

5. The Assembly of United Methodist Women is held once every four years. It is open to every member of United Methodist Women, providing space is available. Eight to twelve thousand women have attended Assemblies in the past. The next Assembly will be held in April 2006 in Anaheim, California. Make plans now for members of your unit to attend and begin to budget for it.

6. Jurisdiction Quadrennial Meetings are held during the final year of the quadrennium. The next meeting will be held in the Spring 2008. The pattern of these varies in the five jurisdictions, so inquire about the meeting in your own jurisdiction.